CHRIST OUR SAVIOUR

T0321850

CHRIST OUR SAVIOUR

Reflections with God

Gary May

ELM HILL

A Division of
HarperCollins Christian Publishing

www.elmhillbooks.com

Christ Our Saviour
Reflections with God

Published in Nashville, Tennessee, by Elm Hill, an imprint of Thomas Nelson. Elm Hill and Thomas Nelson are registered trademarks of HarperCollins Christian Publishing, Inc.

Elm Hill titles may be purchased in bulk for educational, business, fund-raising, or sales promotional use. For information, please e-mail SpecialMarkets@ThomasNelson.com.

Publisher's Note: This novel is a work of fiction. Names, characters, places, and incidents are either products of the author's imagination or used fictitiously. All characters are fictional, and any similarity to people living or dead is purely coincidental.

Library of Congress Cataloging-in-Publication Data

Library of Congress Control Number: 2020902506

ISBN 978-1-400331253 (Paperback)
ISBN 978-1-400331260 (eBook)

Christ Our Saviour

Come quickly they did say to me
It's Jesus, He's at Calvary
Some people look like they are at a loss
As they nailed Him securely to the cross

What has He done? It's just not fair
To see Him nailed and hanging there
He knew no sin, His life was pure
For our sinful lives He had the cure

Why punish Him? He did no wrong!
I think they knew this all along
But even hanging on the cross
His grace shone through, it was our loss

He knew He had to die for us
He suffered for us all without a fuss
He knew the greater plan ahead
And focused on all that instead

Even while He was mocked and spat upon
He knew what would happen when He was gone
And even then amongst His pain
He simply thought of what we'd gain

He did all this for you and me
Why do you find this hard to see?
He gave His life that we might know
The gift of life like He told us so

So don't delay, oh please don't wait
To put your life right, don't hesitate
Jesus did it all, to Him confess
Admit your sin so He can bless

He died for you, your sins He took
He foretold all this in His Holy Book
So don't waste another moment more
Ask Him into your life and He'll come for sure!

God's Wonderful Creation

(December 2018)

As I sit here by the window looking out
I ask is there a God and I have no doubt
I see the leaves blowing gently around
As they fall from the trees unto the ground

My God, He created all of this
There's nothing of Him I want to miss
He created this, 'twas in His plan
How can they say, 'Twas made by man!

Just stop awhile and take it in
Then turn and praise your God within
He created all things good
We need to praise Him as we should

There is no other God like Him
And my life without Him would be so grim
So let us lift our hearts with praise
As with our hearts to Him we gaze

Let us all in the next few days
Spend time with God, do as He says
You'll reap the benefits of drawing near
He'll take your pain and all your fear

O Lord

O Lord to You this prayer I pray
That You would help me through this day
This prayer to You is very real
So to Your heart I do appeal

O Lord I do appreciate
You fill my heart with love, not hate
Help me to be what You desire
And fill my heart with Holy Fire

O Lord I thank You for the greatest love
A love that comes from You above
I know that without You I'm lost
But to know You came at Your great cost

O Lord I find it hard to see
How You could love someone like me
I've criticized, I've let You down
But thank You Lord, You're still around

O Lord I want to move with You
And do the things You want me to
I know the walk ahead is tough
But Your great love will be enough

O Lord I know you make it clear
That Your great love casts out all fear
So why then to You must I admit
That I am afraid of quite a bit?

O Lord please give me confidence
To never sit upon the fence
To stand for You, no matter what
And to share with others what I've got

THE CONVERSION OF SAUL

The first time he was mentioned was in Acts 7:58;
He wasn't filled with love, in fact was filled with hate
He went around to every Church and entered every house
His aim was very simple, the Christian lives to douse

He was a man that Satan used to persecute the Church
It would have to be an answered prayer to knock him off his perch
His name was firstly mentioned as Stephen was stoned to death
It didn't seem to bother him at Stephen's final breath

Then came the day that changed his life, a better man to be
He was travelling to Damascus when he found he couldn't see
He heard the Lord as He spoke to him, his eyes blinded by the light
His heart was full of fear, oh yes it gave him quite a fright!

He knew that he would have to do exactly as 'twas told
Was this a sign of weakness from a man who was so bold?
To Damascus he was told to go, the Lord knew who he'd meet
God then spoke to Ananias to tell him of the feat

You must arise yourself and go to the street called Straight
For I am sending Saul from Tarsus, he has come to meet his fate
Are You sure Ananias asked Him, haven't You heard about this man?
Of course I have, God told him, but he's a vessel in My plan

So Ananias went as he was told to meet the evil Saul
He tried to go with open heart, obedience was his goal
He found the house where Saul was at and laid his hands on him as told
If it wasn't for the words God spoke would he have been so bold?

Immediately what looked like scales fell from the eyes of Saul
Saul knew at once the change he felt as he received the call
His life would change forever, of that there'd be no doubt
Instead of persecuting man, "Praise God" would be his shout!

As he received his sight again, and with the Holy Spirit filled
I guess that he was nervous, but I bet that he was thrilled!
He arose and got himself baptized as time was of the essence
This man was changed at once by God and had the Holy Spirit's presence

He preached Christ in the Synagogues, the people were amazed
Even when they sought to kill him, he did not avert his gaze
He kept his eyes on Jesus as the disciples helped him flee
From the Jews who planned to kill him, these people couldn't see

This man of God wrote many letters to the Churches all around
These letters stood the test of time because they're very sound
He taught the Churches many things, in the ways and things of God
I just hope that this poetic verse has given your life a prod

Saul gave his life to God and then had it turned around
And He can do the same for you, God's waiting to be found
So don't hesitate to give your life to Him who'll always be
For God is so dependable, take that from Saul and me!

THE LOST SHEEP

Which one of you could go to sleep
If you had lost one of your sheep?
I'm sure that Shepherd didn't count the cost
For the thing that mattered was the sheep he lost

Ok you say, he still had ninety-nine
But he started with a hundred, that's the bottom line!
Yes he may have lost one little Ewe
Would that mean anything to me or you?

The Shepherd left those ninety-nine
Would I have done that if they were mine?
He went back to search for that sheep
Until he found it he wouldn't sleep

He finally found it, he couldn't help but weep
For he had found his hundredth and missing sheep
He put it on his shoulders to carry him back
Now he had a hundred and nothing was lack

He took it back, he rejoiced all the way
He had to tell everyone what had happened that day
He told friends and neighbours of how he felt the pain
Which didn't leave him until he found it again

Are you like the sheep feeling lost and afraid
Jesus loves you and the price He has already paid
He died on the cross and gave His life up for you
For He was the only One who could pay what was due

Are you the sheep that went astray?
Well you can change all that if you want today!
Jesus is the Shepherd who is calling to you
He loves you and wants to make your life anew

(27 February 2013)

The Woman Caught in Adultery in John 8:1–11

Jesus came down from the Mount of Olives that day
To the Temple to share and to give and to pray
The people came forward for they knew He'd be there
So He sat down and taught them for He had plenty to share

An Adulteress was brought to the Temple by men
Then said to Jesus, "What would you do with her then?"
They said, "Teacher, we saw her, she was caught in the act!"
They brought her to Jesus to see how He'd react.

They quoted Moses to Him and what was said in the Law
You can't argue with that for we have witnesses who saw
What do You say, they said, testing Him there
Jesus knew what they were saying, He was very aware

Jesus' reaction to them as they all started to linger
Was to draw on the sand using only a finger
What He wrote we don't know, it has not been recorded
But the Scribes and the Pharisees were not to be thwarted

They continued to ask Him, they all wanted the worst
He who is without sin among you, let him throw a stone first
That's not what they wanted to hear from this Man
But it was strange how their conscience and convictions began!

One by one from the oldest even to the last
They were convicted of things they had done in the past
When Jesus looked up she was there all alone
For no one was able to throw the first stone

Woman where are those gone who accused you of this?
Has no one condemned you or did all the stones miss?
She said no one has stoned me, although I did wrong
For she was also convicted, but her accusers had gone

Neither do I condemn you He said, Go, and sin no more
What a message to dwell on for each one of us I'm sure
Don't dwell on your sin ask Jesus to forgive you
For He desires a good relationship between Him and you too.

Demons Entering a Herd of Swine, Mark 5:1–17

Jesus came from the lake where He'd just calmed the storm
The disciples were frightened, it was not of the norm
They came to the country, Gadarenes it was called
They were met by a man who shouted and bawled

This man was so strong, chains and shackles couldn't hold
He was so ravaged and hurt, out there in the cold
No one could tame him for he was too strong
The people were worried, should that be so wrong?

They did what they thought right to this man that was wild
For they had families amongst them, what would he do to a Child?
He saw Jesus afar off and ran to Him there
What would Jesus say? Would He really care?

Of course Jesus cared and He knew what to do
If we were in that position would we all know too?
The man cried out to Jesus for he knew who He was
'Twas the demons inside him who were pleading their cause

Jesus cried out, "Come out of this man," this wasn't a game
Then He asked the unclean spirit, "What is your name?"
We are called legion because many are we
Don't send us out of the country they said earnestly

Now a large herd of swine were feeding nearby
Let us enter the swine was the demons' final cry
With Jesus' permission the demons entered the swine
They all ran violently into the sea from the long steep incline

Those who fed the swine fled, they had to go tell
That the man they had feared had indeed been made well
The people they told couldn't believe their own eyes
To see this man well was a tremendous surprise

When they saw with their own eyes what Jesus had done
Of the victory over the demons that Jesus had won
They became very afraid of what happened and so
They turned to the Lord Jesus and told Him to go

Jesus didn't stop to argue or plead for His case
He knew it was time to move on from that place
Do we try to prolong what God's doing through us
Or do we move on without making a fuss?

This miracle of Jesus should therefore help us to see
That He didn't outstay His welcome it's plain there to me
He did what He did and left without fuss or ado
Could we all do that, I mean me and you?

Sometimes we can dwell on the things God has done
And can sometimes forget there's another victory to be won
So don't dwell on the past or the glory that's been had
Look to the next time and make your hearts glad

Feeding the Five Thousand

When Jesus had heard of what happened to John
He decided to leave, on a boat He was gone
Jesus needed to spend some time on His own
To talk to His Father in a place all alone

The multitude sought Him, their Savior to meet
When they heard where He was they took to their feet
There seemed to be thousands as Jesus looked quick
But then filled with compassion He began to heal all the sick

Soon it was evening the disciples thought 'twas best
To tell Jesus to send them all home for some rest
"They have nothing to eat, there's young children here too"
"You feed them," He said, "It'll give you something to do"

All we have here is two loaves and five fish
In all probability it'll make only one dish
It will never be enough for the five thousand we have here
We could probably feed a family, but that's all we do fear

Bring them to Me, was Jesus' word
They brought them to Him, though they thought it absurd
What could He do with so little to share
But what happened next caught them all unaware

Jesus then took the loaves and the fish He was given
He turned to His Father as He looked up to Heaven
Jesus blessed it and broke it and they passed it around
It wasn't just His disciples that He did astound

There were five thousand men besides women and children
Who all ate and were filled by the food they were given
The lad who had given the fish and the bread
Must have felt very pleased, although it's not said

The remains that were left, twelve baskets in all
That's something that happens when God answers your call
If Jesus can feed those five thousand plus
Just think what He can do with a people like us

(16 April 2012)

HEROES

I've never been a hero and have yet to find some fame
I've always wanted to be one but somehow it never came
I sometimes stop and look around at heroes as some would call
And I must admit if they are heroes then I'm an utter fool

Some get hero status just as and when they sing a song
But to me a hero is much more and I feel that they are wrong
To save someone from dying or to put your life on the line for strangers
That's what I call a hero, someone who ignores the dangers

There's many heroes mentioned in God's Holy Word
And to bracket them with pop stars is really quite absurd
To think that God's own chosen few spoke truth to all the world
These people were so often killed as God's truth they all unfurled

There's many I could speak of, such as Stephen, John or Paul
The list would be so endless if I gave mention to them all
But most of all the hero who is obvious to me
Is Jesus, God's own Holy Son who died to set us free

He didn't make excuses when told that He must die
And even at His final breath just gave a little sigh
So when I think of heroes and whether it applies to me
Well when my life is over we'll just have to wait and see

Relax, Let Go, and Let God
Seek the Kingdom of God,
Luke 12:22–31

Jesus told His disciples not to worry or fret
God knows you have needs and with Him they'll be met
He knows you need clothing, He knows you need to be fed
So don't let these things worry you or get into your head

Life means more than the food that you eat
God has said that all your needs He will meet
Clothes for your body is another thing you fear
God has promised to clothe you He made that so clear

He said, "Look at the ravens who neither sow nor do they reap"
But your God knows of your needs so please don't you weep
How much more value are you than a bird
To think God won't feed you, isn't that quite absurd?

What good is worrying? Will that add to your stature?
The more you trust God, the more you'll mature
If you then are not able to do even the least
Why not let God give you the increase?

Consider the Lilies they neither toil or spin
Wouldn't that be a wonderful place to be in!
Even Solomon himself who was clothed in great glory
Couldn't compete with the Lilies so great is God's story

If God clothes the grass that is here today and then gone
How much more will He ensure that you have clothes to put on
But what is the catch? Is that all I need do?
Well almost but God has a requirement from you!

He told us to seek the Kingdom of God first of all
Keep your eyes on Him and beware lest you fall
So what of your life, are you seeking His will?
Are you taking the time to know God and be still?

THE DENIAL OF PETER

Jesus thanked and blessed the wine and the bread
Do this in remembrance of Me He then said
They then went to the Mount of Olives and sung
It was there that He revealed what had to be done

All of you will be made to stumble He said
Not me said Peter! I'd rather be dead
Simon said Jesus, Satan will sift you as wheat
I know you'll deny Me before we next meet

I will not deny You, I will keep on my toes
Jesus said, "You'll deny Me before the cock crows"
Peter spoke what he thought was deep in his heart
Then he watched from a distance as he saw Jesus depart

He first denied Christ to a girl she said knew
That Peter who sat there was one of the few
So when he was asked, I'm afraid he said No!
That was the first of denials before the cock crowed

Now after a while he heard another one say
Isn't he one of them, isn't he of that way?
So yet again Peter denied it because
He was afraid what they'd do if they found out he was

Another hour had passed when another one spoke
I'm sure that I saw him with that Jesus bloke
That Jesus you spoke of, I don't really know
It was then that Christ looked at him and he heard the cock crow

So Peter went off and bitterly cried
For he was reminded of the times he had lied
"I won't deny You! I'd rather be dead"
It was then he remembered what Jesus had said

Oh what have I done! Was his cry from the heart
And if you need forgiveness that's a good place to start
Could Jesus forgive him after what he had done?
Yes, Jesus' death on the cross means that victory is won

So don't be afraid to cry out today
It's what Jesus wants so to him will you pray?
The victory in Jesus has already been done
The price of your sin has already been won

THE PARABLE OF THE TEN VIRGINS

The ten Virgins and lamps is what this is about
You've heard it before, of that I've no doubt
But just to remind you of this Parable
I thought that I'd write of what it did tell

The story is told of ten Virgins at night
Who were told to be ready and have their own light
We know five were foolish and five of them wise
They were told what to do so there'd be no surprise

The five who were foolish didn't bother with their light
If the Bridegroom was coming, He wouldn't come at night
The five who were wise filled their lamps with some oil
Yes it did take them time but to them 'twas no toil

Well we know that the Bridegroom did come in the night
I can imagine the foolish ones grabbing their light
They panicked and asked the wise for some fuel
The wise hadn't enough, they weren't trying to be cruel

The foolish amongst them searched for oil to buy
But when they returned, without a word of a lie
The wise Virgins had gone, they weren't there anymore
When the foolish got back the Bridegroom had closed up the door

The foolish had returned and kicked up a fuss
O come on Lord please open up just for us
We've oil in our lamps, let us come in too
But the Lord's answer assuredly was "I do not know you"

This Parable should be a lesson for us too
To be ready and willing as He calls us to do
Would we be ready? Could we make the vow?
That we would be ready if He did come back NOW!

What Is Christmas to You and Me?

What is Christmas to you and me?
Is it presents, cards and Christmas tree?
There must be more when all is done
When we've ate the food and had some fun

So what else is there besides all this?
Is there something that we all can miss
Yes there is something else amongst all the mirth
It's about the One who was sent from Heaven to earth

Jesus is His name, our Saviour to be
He was sent from God, to save us you see
He was born in a stable, a very humble start
Yet He came to redeem us, to set us apart

He was born very humbly, in a stable that night
A King born in a stable just didn't seem right
Even the Wise men to the Palace appeared
For that's where they thought the King would be reared

The Shepherds in the fields whilst watching their flock
All did what the Angel said but were they in for a shock
There in the stable amongst all the cattle and sheep
Was the Saviour of the world so blissfully asleep

That Child asleep, how hard 'twas to see
Was the Saviour who died for you and for me
His humble beginning stayed with Him all His life here
Is it any wonder why we love Him so dear?

That Child and Man took our sins as He died
Then on the cross "It is finished," He cried
Well that wasn't the end of His life there and then
For that was the start of Him living again

He first conquered hell for you and for me
He then gave us the chance to repent and be free
So don't waste a moment and please don't despair
He's now up in heaven preparing for us there

So now if I ask you, "What is Christmas to you?"
I hope you're reminded of His blessings for you too
My hope is that amongst all the presents you get
Is the most precious of gifts that you'll receive yet

(9 December 2017)

DON'T DELAY, GOD LOVES YOU

As we are gathered here to praise God's Name
And to remember Jesus who took our shame
He hung there on the cross for us
He did this all without a fuss

Why did He do it for you or me
The answer's simple, to set us free
Our lives are full of sin you know
But Jesus died for us, the way to show

Don't think that you don't need Him too
After all that Jesus did for you
He took your pain, He took your sin
So take the time to ask Him in

He wants to be a part of you
He wants to love you through and through
Don't let this opportunity be wasted
Ask someone who has already tasted

(4 December 2013)

GOD'S DESIGN

I thought I'd say a little word
About the things I find absurd
Like having the legs of a centipede
Are you sure a hundred legs they need?

Another thing I just can't see why
The Kiwi has wings but cannot fly
Then I thought about the Giraffe and heck
Why does it need that great long neck

Now what about the garden snail
Who where he goes he leaves a trail
And then there is of course the mole
Who spends his life down in a hole

The Ostrich he is often found
With his head that's buried underground
The Cow does nothing or so it would seem
But she does give us our milk and cream

The Caterpillar must wonder why
It turns into a Butterfly
The Hedgehog we must not forget
Whose needles on his back protect

Now if you care to look around
I'm sure there's others to be found
There's just too many for me to count
God knows how many, the exact amount

Yes, God made them all to His design
His imagination is so much more than mine
So next time you look and think, "That's odd"
Remember who made it and give thanks to God

(31 July 2019)

New Year Poem 2018

As we look forward to the coming New Year
Are you filled with excitement or is it something to fear
So I thought it would be good to address some of our issues
Yes for some perhaps it's time to reach for the tissues

What have we done for God in the year past
Or what has God done for us that had left us aghast?
I'm sure there are things if we stop to reflect
Of when God touched us, our lives to affect

We are probably aware of some unfinished tasks
But don't worry about that if you are doing what God asks
For if we just stop as you are all sat in your seat
Just remember that God's work in us is still incomplete

So please take some heart, you are not all alone
Take it as another year in the Lord you have grown
Let's give our thanks for what God has done
And rejoice over God's grace for the things yet to come

The future for some can be full of worry and stress
But try and relax as God just wants us to be blessed
We aren't all called to be in the front line
Just do as God leads you and you will be fine

Let's take heart from this and encourage one another
Do as God leads you and bless your sister and brother
Then this time next year I'm sure we will see
That He not only blessed you but He also blessed me!

THE BIRTH OF JESUS

Gabriel the angel told Mary to rejoice
God has chosen you, you are His choice
You of all women have been blessed by God
You have been chosen by Him, He's given you the nod

Mary was frightened and you would be too
If God had told you what He was going to do
You will bring forth a child, Jesus will be His name
But Mary was worried as she thought of the shame

I am not married and have not been with a man
But God had already thought of that in His plan
God's Holy Spirit will come upon you
And He will be with you all the way through

Mary told Joseph of all that was said
Joseph started to worry of the things up ahead
He thought in his heart to put her away
That was until the Lord had His say

"Joseph," God said, "Let go of your fears
Mary is pregnant, but it's not what it appears
She has been chosen, the child is of Me
So please understand and in time you will see"

The time soon came around for Mary to give birth
It was the time when a bit of Heaven came down to the earth
The King of all kings in a stable was born
Swaddling cloths were what the Lord Jesus had worn

There were Shepherds out living in fields in the night
When the angel of the Lord gave them all quite a fright
Don't be afraid I bring good tidings of great joy
You must go to Bethlehem to see this new Boy!

He is the Saviour, who is Christ the Lord
So hurry and see Him you have no time to afford
When the angels had gone they spoke to each other
Let's go and find Jesus and Mary His mother

They all went with haste to see what God said
And there they saw Jesus asleep in His bed
When they had seen Him they told what they saw
How they were visited by an angel and were all left in awe

The next to be told were wise men from the east
But to me they didn't seem wise in the least
They headed to the best places where they thought He'd be
They didn't understand, they just couldn't see

Jesus was born in a stable you see
So He could relate to you and to me
If He was born in a Palace so fair
Would we be able to relate to Him there?

So as we consider this time of the year
Let's be like the shepherds and let us draw near
To the Lord who has called us to follow Him through
Do you feel in your heart that He's calling you too?

(14 December 2013)

THE LORD'S GLORY AND MAJESTY

(January 2019)

As we look around this world
We see what You, the Lord unfurled
We see your Splendour around us each day
You are perfect Lord in every way

You are Majestic in holiness and awesome in glory
We need to tell the world of your story
You are still working wonders today as You have been
Your wonders are still with us, they are there to be seen

You're a God of great mercy, we don't deserve it
You gave us Your Word and we need to observe it
We are so relieved that You don't stay angry forever
And we praise You and thank You, You brought us together

You Lord are great, Yours is the glory and power
Please show us Your splendour at this very hour
Your Way God is perfect and we're really blessed
We thank You for loving us as You are the best

THE STORY OF JONAH

Jonah was a righteous man, he loved God through and through
Until that was when God revealed, what He wanted him to do
Arise said God and then, to Nineveh you must go
But Jonah set off to Tarshish hoping the Lord just wouldn't know

So off to Tarshish Jonah went, hoping to flee away
But it wasn't long before a storm arose and caused the boat to sway
The Mariners aboard the boat cried out to their gods in fear
But of course they had no answer back as their boat they couldn't steer

'Twas then they spotted Jonah, fast asleep down in the boat
Awake they said to him and ask your God to help us float
They then decided to cast lots to see who was to blame
So when all the lots were cast it came up with Jonah's name

They fired off questions to him of who and what and why
They thought because of what he did that they all were going to die
The men became all nervous and exceedingly afraid
Because the sin of Jonah seemed also on them laid

I am to blame, Jonah said, I admit that it was me
So the Mariners took hold of him and threw him in the sea
Immediately they threw him in, the raging storm did cease
And all around they experienced total calm and peace

Now this for Jonah was not the quite the end
For a great fish was what the Lord then did send
It swallowed poor Jonah without any bites
And that's where he stayed for three days and three nights

Now Jonah cried out to the Lord in his pain
And told God how he wouldn't make that error again
You see he thought he'd been cast from God's sight
And I can understand why that gave him a fright

After all Jonah's pleading and talking so grand
God spoke to the fish and it spewed Jonah onto land
Now for the second time, God said to Nineveh you must go
And despite all his fears Jonah just couldn't say no

So off to Nineveh Jonah finally went
And he probably thought of the last days that he spent
How he prayed to God while he was in despair
And how God answered him, even in there!

The best thing that happened was that Nineveh repented
Then God from His plan to destroy them relented
But even in this Jonah still had a moan
And if I was God I would have left him alone!

Now that is the beauty of God don't you see
God just said is it right for you to be angry?
Jonah then made a shelter on the east of the city
And there he dwelt amongst his self-pity

Is it right for you to rave and rant
Are you indeed angry about this here plant?
The Lord said you have pity for the plant you didn't grow
So why can't you be happy for the grace I did show?

So now as we sit back and reflect on this true story
Let's sit back and think about God and His Glory
The people of Nineveh turned around and repented
So from the disaster He planned, He later relented

Now let this be a lesson to me and to you
To just let God do what He's planning to do
Don't be like Jonah and go your own way
Surrender to God without any delay!

God will be with you through thick and through thin
So open your heart and let God come in
I know that you'll have no regrets from that day
Just open your heart and then to Him pray

What Is It Lord That I Must Do?

What is it Lord that I must do?
To know if Your Word is really true
I hear them say, "Your Word is truth"
But I can't help feeling I need some proof

What is it Lord that I must do?
I hear them say, "He'll speak to you"
You'll know His voice, you'll know His will
But the times I've heard Him equals nil

What is it Lord that I must do
To get my life so right with you
It seems so hard to me right now
Please help me Lord, today somehow

There are so many things to ask
But I think these questions are just a mask
For when all I ask is said and done
There's only one answer, accept your Son

That's it Lord, that's what I must do
To know you in me through and through
I must repent, turn away from sin
And throw my old life in the bin

How foolish of me all along
To think in my ways I was strong
Now I look to You, so full of Truth
O, thank You Lord I have the proof

I thank You now Lord for Your Word
Which once I thought was so absurd
I thank You Lord that it's so real
And I can feast on it, a ready meal

O Lord I now can hear Your voice
At last I finally can rejoice
It was not through anything I did
It was You who lifted off my lid

Now as I walk with You each day
A simple prayer to You I pray
That in everything I say or do
I'll be a witness Lord for you

www.ingramcontent.com/pod-product-compliance
Ingram Content Group UK Ltd.
Pitfield, Milton Keynes, MK11 3LW, UK
UKHW031124120325
456135UK00006B/146